THE SONG THE OWL GOD SANG

The collected Ainu legends of Chiri Yukie

Translated into English by Benjamin Peterson

Published by BJS Books (www.okikirmui.com)

Cover and book design by Creative Sciences

Cover created using Serious Paint (www.seriouspaint.com)

Cover image © Tomo.Yun (www.yunphoto.net/en/)

Heartfelt thanks to:

The Camborne Celtic Collective for their support

The staff at Creative Sciences and BJS Books

The members of Project Okikirmui

Tamura Suzuko for her excellent *Ainu-Japanese Dictionary*

Hideo Kirikae for his excellent *Lexicon of the Ainu Shinyoushuu*

TABLE OF CONTENTS

About Chiri Yukie   i

About the Book   iii

About this Translation   v

Prologue   1

The Song The Owl God Sang   3

The Song The Fox Sang   13

The Song The Black Fox Sang   19

The Song The Rabbit Sang   25

The Song The Marsh Demon Sang   29

The Song The Wolf Cub Sang   33

The Song The Owl God Sang: "Konkuwa"   37

The Song The Sea God Sang   43

The Song The Frog Sang   51

A Song Pon Okikirmui Sang   53

Another Song Pon Okikirmui Sang   55

The Song The Otter Sang   59

The Song The Mussel Sang   61

About Chiri Yukie

Hours before her sudden death at the age of nineteen, Chiri Yukie completed her only book, *Ainu Shinyoushuu,* a collection of traditional chants in the Ainu language.

Her book, written in parallel Ainu and Japanese text, was the first book in or about the Ainu language to be written from the point of view of an actual Ainu speaker. It was also arguably the first ever printed literary work from a shamanistic culture.

Chiri Yukie at 18

The Ainu, the original inhabitants of Sakhalin and Hokkaido, have a language and culture very different from the Siberian cultures of the mainland and from their Japanese neighbors. This language and culture did not suffer the almost total annihilation that befell many of the original cultures of northeast Asia. Protected by their island location and long (though very unequal) relationship with Japan, at the beginning of the twentieth century the Ainu population of Hokkaido still retained their architecture, religion, and oral literature.

Chiri Yukie (Chiri is the family name) was born in 1903, at a time when Hokkaido was being rapidly developed and modernized, transitioning from Japanese domination to Japanese assimilation.

Traditional Ainu customs such as bear sacrifice and tattooing were ending, urbanization was proceeding rapidly, and Ainu populations were ill-equipped to assert themselves against a vigorous Japanese culture which was itself rapidly taking on Western characteristics and which regarded the 'primitive' natives of Hokkaido as something of a detail.

Chiri was born to an aristocratic but impoverished Ainu family; though her father had been a chief, for financial reasons she was adopted and brought up by her aunt and her grandmother. Both these women were well versed in the oral tradition, which at that time had already begun to break down for lack of storytellers. One day, the Japanese linguist Kindaichi Kyousuke visited the three and explained his work; Chiri then decided to devote herself to recording her aunt's stories, transcribing them into Roman characters with her own method and translating them into Japanese.

At the age of nineteen, she travelled to Tokyo, having prepared a set of thirteen of her aunt's *yukar*, a type of chanted fable. Briefly, she worked with Kindaichi to prepare what should have been the first of many anthologies. On the day it was finished, she died suddenly from heart failure.

Soon after her death, her book was published unaltered by Kindaichi. With its clear and elegant colloquial Japanese rendition, it achieved great success, generating great interest in what had previously been seen as a minor footnote to the colonization of Hokkaido. Later scholars, including members of Chiri's family, went on to extensively record and popularize the Ainu oral literature, and today the Ainu text she wrote can still be understood by those who learn Ainu as a second language.

The result is a unique window into an Asian shamanistic poetic tradition – one of many that once existed, but one of very few to be studied and recorded while still largely alive.

ABOUT THE BOOK

Ainu oral tradition encompasses many forms and many regional variations. Stories are divided into categories, each associated with a type of subject matter and a mode of recital. The categorization varies greatly between regions but there are three overarching types.

Wepeker are folk tales told in prose and in ordinary language.

Yukar are epics about human heroes and their deeds, traditionally sung by men.

Kamui yukar are tales chanted in the first person by gods (*kamui*), spirits, animals, objects, and personifications of natural forces. These are the tales that Chiri yukie collected.

Kamui yukar is a form with many fixed characteristics. They are chanted to a short, repetitive tune. A refrain called a *sakehe* begins the tale and is repeated at intervals; sometimes this refrain forms part of the story but often it consists of syllables whose meaning is unknown. The *sakehe* is unique to a given tale, and serves as a title. It can be repeated frequently throughout the recitation, forming part of the metric structure; in these written versions, the *sakehe* is used less often.

The language of *kamui yukar* is formal and archaic. The tale is always the first person account of a *kamui*, a god or spirit, and always ends with a declaration of the form '...this was the song such and such a god sung about himself'. Where human heroes come into the narrative, they may be represented as children.

As well as restrictions on the form, the subject matter of *kamui yukar* has many patterns and subdivisions. Some relate to nature and animal spirits; *The Song the Frog Sang* is one of these. Another type relates to major, named spirits that are more like gods; *The*

Song the Owl God Sang is in this category. These tales often explain and reinforce social customs such as the use of *inau*, sticks of shaved wood used in interactions with the *kamui*.

Particularly in this collection, an overarching theme is the close relationship between the human world, *ainu moshir*, and the spirit world, *kamui moshir*. Ainu culture involved a very close everyday relationship between the physical and the intangible; the layout of houses, the patterns of clothing, the tattoos with which women were adorned from childhood, the ubiquitous *inau*, the rituals of hunting, feasting and sacrifice were all physical signs of mankind's dependency on the goodwill of the spirit world and were all required in order to maintain that goodwill.

The detail and pragmatism of this relationship is hard to picture now. For example, when hunting bear, there was an implied arrangement between the human hunters and the *kamui* within the bear. But this arrangement was not a simple exchange; it was a formal and complex multi-way agreement. Major *kamui* such as Apehuchi the hearth goddess played their roles and required their dues, and these roles could be complicated. Tracking dogs were messengers from Apehuchi who would invite Kimun Kamui, the god of mountains, to send a bear, which would then be shot with aconite-poisoned arrows. The *kamui* of the aconite plant could be seen as beautiful women who persuaded the *kamui* of the bear into accepting the invitation. The mere act of gathering the aconite to make poison involved offering beer and *inau* to four other *kamui*.

Chiri Yukie's tales do not focus on the details, but paint a vivid picture of the vital balance and commerce between the two worlds. If one wishes to have fish to eat, it seems, one must remember to look beyond the fish to the *kamui* within it.

ABOUT THIS TRANSLATION

Translating Chiri Yukie's parallel Ainu and Japanese text into English is perhaps not quite so hard as Chiri's original translation from Ainu into Japanese, but it still presents many challenges and many inevitable compromises.

First and foremost, the Ainu text is meant to be sung, not read; *yukar* are recited to a short repeating melody and with a specific intonation that cannot be expressed in English text. I have tried to retain the sense that this is a poetic form by breaking the lines, as far as possible, where Chiri Yukie did. However, even in the Japanese text, the metre is irretrievably lost. The first line of each *yukar* gives the *sakehe*, the refrain, which is usually untranslatable, and so has usually been left exactly as written in Ainu.

Secondly, the Ainu language in which these *yukar* were written down is not particularly in line with modern concepts. The vocabulary is not particularly extensive, but on each word and phrase there may tower a cargo of meaning and allusion. One of the most remarkable things about Chiri's original translation is the relationship between the clear, sophisticated, beautiful Japanese text and the superficially simpler original.

For example, human beings in the original are referred to almost invariably simply as *ainu*; this may mean 'human', 'Ainu', 'person', 'inhabitant' and so on. The word *nispa* refers to an unusually important person and may mean 'chief', 'wealthy man', 'honored ancestor' as the case may be. *Kamui* is normally translated 'god', but 'spirit' or even 'demon' can often be more appropriate. Both the Japanese text and this translation, therefore, use many different words where the Ainu original uses only one; this is one of the ways in which a translator's culture inevitably imposes itself on a text.

Other words are problematic because of the great weight of cultural reference that rests on them. The best example is *inau*. An *inau* is a shaved willow wand with a tuft of bark strips at one end. The general significance of *inau* can be inferred to some extent from these stories – they are ritual objects which *kamui* are fond of. But in fact there is a great wealth of detail around different types of *inau* and the places they are kept and the occasions on which they are used, that does not directly appear in this book, and the same goes for the different parts of the house and the objects found in the house. The result is that some passages can seem rather arbitrary and terse in English. The translator must turn, feebly, to the use of footnotes.

Other expressions are difficult for yet other reasons. The fox's song, for example, contains some rude words whose exact nuance is unclear to me. I have rendered these in English with what I hope are approximately similar rude words. Chiri Yukie on the other hand chose to use delicate and adorable Japanese euphemisms.

Lastly, and here I must offer my own apologies, translation is difficult. Even the translation from Ainu to Japanese has some unclear points – how much more so my hit-or-miss rendition into English. This translation has many faults and weaknesses, which the reader is warmly invited to highlight, criticize, and fix.

CHIRI YUKIE'S PROLOGUE

Long ago, this broad land of Hokkaido was a world in which our ancestors lived lives of freedom. Like children of unspoilt innocence, they lived their carefree lives in the embrace of mother Nature, whose beloveds they were – what happy people they must have been!

In winter, kicking aside the thick snow that covered field and forest, hunting the bear across mountain after mountain in defiance of the frost that froze all the world – on the summer ocean, in the cool wind, swimming the green waves, setting sail, under the cries of the white seagulls, in little leaf-like boats to seek fish – in the flower-filled spring, bathing in the gentle sunlight, singing along with the endlessly-warbling birds, plucking sagebrush and butterbur – in the red-leafed Fall, splitting the ripe ears of grain, not extinguishing till midnight the salmon-fishing fires, hearing the deer cry to one another in the ravine, falling, beneath the round moon, into a dream-laden slumber. Oh, what a wonderful way of life it must have been! That tranquil state of mind is already a thing of the past, a dream torn apart by the passing decades, for this earth is changing quickly, with hills and meadows becoming villages and villages becoming cities one after another.

Somehow, almost unnoticed, the form that Nature had worn in ancient times began to fade, and of the people who once dwelt so happily in field and mountain, most are no longer to be found. The few of us who remain of our race do nothing but stare in astonishment at the way the world has gone. Yet what we see from these eyes is that the radiance of the beautiful spirits of our forebears, whose every gesture was ruled by a sense of the spiritual, has been burdened with unease, consumed with discontent, weakened, dizzied, become helpless, gone beyond the reach of outside help, a miserable sight, something doomed to annihilation... Such is the name we have now – what a sad name it is that we now bear.

Our happy ancestors of long ago – it must have been impossible for them to imagine that in the end their native land would decay to this wretched state.

Time flows ever on, the world endlessly goes on changing. If from the worthless remnant who still exist on the site of our great defeat, there could someday emerge just two or three strong leaders, then perhaps the day when we catch up again with the changing world might not be far off. That is our true cherished wish, for which we pray morning and night.

But... the language that we use each day to share our feelings with our beloved ancestors has become worn with use. Even the beautiful words that have been handed down to us are mostly timid things, things which will surely be extinguished along with their weak, doomed users. Oh, what a heartbreaking thing – and almost already only a memory.

I, born an Ainu and living among Ainu speakers, in my spare moments, in rainy evenings and snowy nights, have put together with my clumsy brush just one or two of the very least of the tales our ancestors told for amusement. If it should turn out that this work is read by some who are kind enough to understand us, then I shall share with our race's ancestors joy without limit, happiness unsurpassable.

The Song The Owl God Sang

This beautiful *yukar* is perhaps the single best-known passage of Ainu literature. The narrator is the *hayokpe*, or animal body, of the owl god Chikap Kamui, god of the land and of wealth, whose tears were sometimes considered to be gold and silver. The owl itself is only *hayokpe*, armor worn by Chikap Kamui; when the owl is shot down with an arrow, Chikap Kamui continues his work.

This is one of many *kamui yukar* that stress the importance of a humble attitude and correct rituals from mankind, in exchange for a continued food supply from the *kamui*.

> *"Silver drops fall all around, golden drops fall all around"*
> I sang as I glided above a stream and over a village,
> And as I passed I gazed down –
> Those who had been poor had become rich,
> Those who had been rich were now poor, it seemed.
> On the beach, human children were playing
> With toy arrows and toy bows.[1]
> "Silver drops fall all around,
> Golden drops fall all around,"
> I sang as I flew over the children
> And they ran below me and said:
>
> "Beautiful bird! Divine bird!
> Let's shoot arrows at that bird
> The one who hits the divine bird, the one who gets it first
> Is a true hero, a true champion!"

---

[1] Ainu boys were usually given toy bows and arrows at a certain age, so that by shooting at trees and birds they would learn archery. [Chiri]

So saying, the children of those who had been poor
And were now rich
Putting gold arrows to their gold bows
Shot at me in turn with their gold arrows
Which I caused to pass below me and above me.

In the middle of that group,
One particular boy moved among them
With only an ordinary bow and ordinary arrows.
He seemed to be from a poor family; I could tell
From his clothes. But from his eyes[2]
I understood that he was descended from noble ancestors,
Out of place in such company. He too took his ordinary bow
And ordinary arrows and aimed at me, and
The children of those who had been poor and were now rich
Laughed loudly and said:

"You filthy pauper,
That bird, the divine bird which
Would not take our golden arrows, do you seriously think
It will touch some peasant's ordinary arrows,
Like your arrows of rotting wood?"[3]

So saying, they kicked the poor urchin
And beat him. However, the boy
Ignored them completely and took aim at me.

_____

[2] It was thought that the best way of determining someone's quality was to look into their eyes so a steady gaze was greatly valued. [Chiri]

[3] It was believed that birds and beasts allowed themselves to be shot because they wanted man-made arrows. Being shot down, therefore, is no great disaster for the owl god and in fact is an essential point of commerce between *kamui* and humans. For much of this story, the owl is therefore actually dead, but this is not important from the Ainu point of view

Seeing this, I was filled with pity for him.
"Silver drops fall all around,
Golden drops fall all around,"
I sang as in the sky
I flew in slow circles. The boy,
Taking up an archer's stance,
Biting his lower lip, took aim,
And loosed the arrow. The little arrow flew well,
It reached me, and with my hand
I reached out and received that little arrow.
I spiralled downward, the air rushing past me;
I plummeted to the ground.
Then the boys came running
Raising a blizzard of dust they raced each other.
As I touched the ground, the poor boy
Reached me first and gathered me up,
And those who had been poor but were now rich
Came running after him,
Heaping on him innumerable insults
Pushing him and hitting him:

"You nasty brat, you little jerk
We were about to do that ourselves
And you cut in front of us!"

They said as the poor boy covered me
Under his clothes and fastened me against his body.
After a bitter struggle he found a gap in the crowd,
Jumped through it and made his escape.

Those who had been poor but were now rich
Threw stones and bits of wood, but
The boy ignored them, and
Raising a blizzard of dust he ran until

He arrived outside a little house.
He put me in at the east window,[4] and then
With well-chosen words, fluently told his tale.
From inside the house, an old couple
Came along, raising their hands up over their eyes.[5]
To look at them they were obviously terribly poor
Yet they had a gentlemanly and a ladylike quality.
They were startled to see me and bowed deeply;
Respectfully adjusting their sashes
They petitioned me thus:

"Great owl god,
You favor us by appearing at the inadequate hut
Of mere peasants; accept our thanks.
Once we were counted among the wealthy and great,
And although now we are reduced to these straits,
Mere paupers, in times past the local gods
Often graced our home with their presence;
Therefore, as today's sun
Has already gone down, tonight allow us
To shelter you, Great God, though tomorrow
We can offer you nothing more than an *inau*."

With such pleas they beseeched me time and time again.
Then the old couple, spreading a carpet there,
Placed me by the east window.
Then, everyone lay down, and soon
With resounding snores they all fell asleep.
I sat there between the ears of my earthly body[6]

---

[4] The east window was a sacred part of an Ainu house and not used merely for looking through. It is thus a suitable entry point for the dead owl.

[5] A gesture of humble greeting. [Chiri]

[6] The owl god is within a *hayokpe* (literally 'armor'). In their own world, Ainu deities such as the owl god had a human form and lived in houses. On trips to the

But before long, when midnight came,
I arose.
"Silver drops fall all around,
Golden drops fall all around,"
I sang quietly,
As from the left side of the house to the right,[7]
With beautiful sounds, I flew.
As I beat my wings, around me
Exquisite jewels fell, the divine jewels
Making lovely sounds as they scattered around.
In a moment, that little house was filled
With magnificent treasures, with divine treasures.
"Silver drops fall all around,
Golden drops fall all around,"
I sang as, in one moment, I made that little house
Into a house of gold; I remade into a manor,
A storehouse of magnificent jewels, I quickly transformed it
Into a house adorned with the beauty of magnificent clothes.
Far more splendidly than the house of a lord
I decorated the interior of this mansion. When I had finished
I went back and sat, just as before,
Between the ears of the body I wore.
I caused the people in the house to dream

---

human world, they wore animal forms called *hayokpe*. Even if the animal form died, the *kamui* could remain within it, located between the ears. From a human point of view, then, the owl is dead, but the Ainu know that the *kamui* may well actually still be residing in the body.

[7] Ainu houses had a hearth in the middle, and a 'high seat' by the east window. Looking from this seat, the house could be divided into left and right sides. Only men could sit in the eastern area, and those inferior to the house's owner were barred. The women of the household lined up along the right hand side. Next in the pecking order was the left side. The west side of the house, nearest the door, was the lowliest. [Chiri]

About the Ainu *nispa*,[8] how their luck had failed
And the people who had been poor but were now rich
Laughed at them and tormented them, and how I,
Seeing that, pitied them, and as I am no mere wicked spirit
I came to their human house
And stayed and granted them my blessing – of these things
I informed them.
When that was done, the night gave way to dawn and
The people in the house all got up
And they all saw the inside of the house and rubbed their eyes
And fainted near-lifeless to the floor. The old woman
Cried loudly and the old man
Spilled large tears one after another
But before long they brought themselves before me and
With innumerable prostrations they spoke thus:

"We thought that we merely dreamed, that we merely slept,
But in fact, you were doing all this for us.
At our humble, rustic dwelling
Merely by appearing you greatly favored us,
Great God of the Land, and then
You condescended to take pity on our ill luck,
Piling upon one blessing another still greater."

Speaking through their tears
They addressed me
And then, cutting some wood for an *inau*,
The old couple made a charming new *inau*
And adorned me with it.
The old lady made new clothes;
The boy helped, gathering wood

---

[8] *Nispa* is an important, wealthy or great person. Chiri Yukie usually translated this with various words such as 'chief' but in this line she left it it its Ainu form. Here it may mean 'the greatest among the people'.

Drawing water and preparing sake;
He made preparations, and in a moment
Six barrels of sake were lined up before the high seat.
Then, I called the old hearth goddess,[9] and
Spoke with the various gods.
Two days passed, and already the scent
Of sake (a particular favorite of the gods!)
Drifted in the air.
Then, I made the boy resume his dishevelled appearance
And put on his old clothes and I sent him
Through the village to give invitations to
Those who had been poor and were now rich.
He entered every house and
Proclaimed my message and
Those who had been poor and were now rich
Laughed hugely:

"Well, this is a wonder, the paupers have
Got some sort of sake,
Scraped together some sort of feast,
And it looks like they're inviting everyone.
We should go and have a look at their feeble efforts.
It'll be good for a laugh."

So saying amongst themselves, they gathered in a crowd
And along they came, gathering from miles around;
Just seeing the house
They were so shocked that some instantly returned home
While others got quite close before collapsing, stunned, on the ground.
Then, the old wife went outside
And took their hands and led everyone into the house
But they crawled abjectly along the ground

---

[9] Apehuchi, 'Fire Grandmother', goddess of the hearth and of fire in general. [Chiri]

And not one of them would lift up his face.
Then, the old husband made his appearance
And in a voice as clear as a cuckoo's he spoke.
He spoke of many things:

"When we were poor, it was impossible for us
To come and go freely like this, but
The Great God took pity on us,
Because we entertained no wicked thoughts;
And therefore we were blessed.
From now on to all the village, we will be like family,
We will let bygones be bygones
And everyone who wishes may
Visit us freely."

This speech he set forth, and the people
(Humbly wringing their hands again and again)
Apologized for their ill-treatment, and from now on,
They all declared, they would live as friends.
Everyone joined in worshipping me.
When that was finished, everyone with a glad heart
Began the luxurious banquet.
While chatting with the fire goddess and the house god,[10]
And the old goddess of the household altar[11], I watched them
Dancing their human dances and leaping about
And an amusing sight I found it.
In this way two or three days passed and the party ended.

---

[10] Chisekor Kamui, the god of the house, also called the 'Old man of the House'. [Chiri]

[11] Nusakor Kamui, the goddess of the domestic altar, i.e. of the place where *inau* are kept. In emergencies she may appear to humans, but in the form of a snake. Thus, when a snake is seen in the vicinity of the altar or the east window, people say "Doubtless Grandma Nusakorkamui is going out on an errand," and such a snake is never killed. To do so would invite an unspeakable punishment. [Chiri]

Seeing that good relations prevailed among the humans,
I was contented
And took my leave of the fire goddess,
The house god and the goddess of the altar.
When that was done, I went back to my own house.
By the time I got home, my house was full
Of lovely *inau* and the best sake.
Then I sent messengers to all the gods both near and far
I invited them to a bountiful banquet
And furthermore, to all the gods
I told the tale, of the time I visited the human village,
And of the situation there, and everything that happened,
And they heaped praise on me.
When they went home, I gave to each
Two or even three beautiful *inau*.
Looking at the people of that Ainu village,
Now all at peace, and the people
All living in harmony, and the *nispa*
Once again at the head of the village,
I see that boy, now already grown up,
With a wife of his own and a child too
Who respects both his father and his mother,
And from now on, forever, when he has made sake,
Or at the start of the banquet, he sends me *inau* and sake.
I watch over the people
Forever
I protect the world of humans.

Such was the tale the Owl God told.

THE SONG THE FOX SANG

The second *kamui yukar* makes a change of pace and reflects the earthy sense of humor common in Ainu tradition. It is still, however, a *kamui yukar* rather than a comic song.

Towa towa to!
One day I went out
To look for food by the sea.

Hopping among the stones, *towa towa to*!
Hopping among the twigs, *towa towa to*!
And as I went along what I saw in front of me looked like this:
On the beach a whale had been washed up
And humans were dressed up in fine clothes
Dancing and singing to celebrate the sea's bounty,
And some cut the meat,
And some carried it back and forth,
And the *nispa* recited their prayers of gratitude.[12]
And there were others who sharpened the knives,
And the beach was black with them.
And seeing all that I was ecstatic!
"Oho, I've got to get there quickly
And beg a bit – nothing wrong with that!"
I thought, and yelling "*Onnono! Onnono!*"[13]

---

[12] It was believed that when whales were washed up on the coast, they were thrown up onto the shore by the sea god specifically for the benefit of humans. Therefore, on such occasions august persons would dress in the finest clothes and, facing the sea, give ritual thanks. For the first of three times, the impetuous fox mistakes something quite different for Ainu ritual gestures.

[13] The cry used by Ainu hunters when returning from a successful hunt. [Chiri]

Hopping among the stones, *towa towa to*!
Hopping among the twigs, *towa towa to*!
I ran and I ran and I got a close look
And it wasn't like I'd thought at all.
Cause the thing I thought was a beached whale
Was actually a great big heap of dog shit on the beach
Yes, a mountain of enormous turds
That's what the thing turned out to be
That I thought was a whale.
What I thought were people dancing and singing
And cutting up the meat and so forth
Were actually crows
Having fun among the shit on every side –
I was furious.

"Blind moron
Myopic idiot
Stink-bottomed fool
Smelly-assed twit
Incontinent oaf
What on earth was I thinking?"

And then once more
Hopping among the stones, *towa towa to*!
Hopping among the twigs, *towa towa to*!
I turned slightly inland
And what I saw in front of me looked like this:
There was a boat, and in that boat
There were two people, who were offering condolences to each
other.
"Oho, this must mean
There's been a horrible disaster
Maybe it's a shipwreck or something

Oh, I've got to get there quickly
And hear what's wrong!"
I thought, and yelling "*Hokokes!*"[14]
Hopping among the stones, *towa towa to*!
Hopping among the twigs, *towa towa to*!
I rushed over there like the wind and saw that really
What I thought was a boat was a rocky outcrop and
What I thought were people were two outsize pelicans.
And when these two big pelicans stretched their necks
It looked sort of like two people consoling each other –
At least to me.

"Blind moron
Myopic idiot
Stink-bottomed fool
Smelly-assed twit
Incontinent oaf
What on earth was I thinking?"

And then once more
Hopping among the stones, *towa towa to*!
Hopping among the twigs, *towa towa to*!
I ran, and I turned to go up the river
And directly upstream I saw two women
Standing in the shallows and weeping together.
I was quite shocked.
"Oho, something sad has happened
Someone has brought news of a death
And they're clinging together in grief[15]

---

[14] The cry used by Ainu men to call on divine aid during disasters. [Chiri]

[15] News of a death was carried from village to village by a special messenger, the *ashurkorkur*, whose title means 'the one whose speech is mixed up'. The messenger would cry "*Hokokes!*" and announce the news in purposefully distorted speech. The local women might exchange hugs and tears in the ritual called *uchishkar* – this is the conclusion the fox jumps to when he sees the swaying poles.

Oh, I've got to get there quickly
And hear all the gossip,"
I thought, and
Hopping among the stones, *towa towa to*!
Hopping among the twigs, *towa towa to*!
I rushed, and when I got there I saw that really
There were two poles for holding fish-traps
Standing in the river, shaking with the current
And honestly they looked just like women shaking with tears.

"Blind moron
Myopic idiot
Stink-bottomed fool
Smelly-assed twit
Incontinent oaf
What on earth was I thinking?"

And then I went on upstream
Hopping among the stones, *towa towa to*!
Hopping among the twigs, *towa towa to*!
And ran like the wind all the way home.
But this is what I saw in front of me:
My house was on fire and smoke rose into the sky
A column of smoke like a thundercloud.
Seeing that, I was so horrified
I panicked completely. Screaming like a woman[16]
I leaped toward my house – from which
Someone else called back at me and ran to my side.
Taking a careful look, I realized it was my wife.
"Gracious me, darling," she said, breathless with worry,

---

[16] It isn't mere panic that makes the fox scream like a woman. In times of disaster, Ainu men called on the gods as loudly as possible; but women, with their more piercing voices, could make much softer sounds and still get a response. In times of trouble, therefore, men would imitate women in order to be better heard by the *kamui*. It is to this measure that the desperate fox resorts. [Chiri]

"Whatever's the matter?"
So I took a closer look around and I realized
Although I thought I'd seen my house on fire
There it was still looking about the same as ever.
There was no fire or smoke.
It turned out my wife had been pounding grain
And the winnowed husks of millet
Were what I'd thought was smoke.
I'd gone out looking for food but I still had none,
And worse yet, when I'd shouted so loudly,
My wife jumped with surprise and the grain she was pounding
Went flying off in the wind along with the husks.
And the result was that I had nothing at all to eat.
And I was so furious I threw myself to the floor
Crashed to the ground, and just lay there.

"Blind moron
Myopic idiot
Stink-bottomed fool
Smelly-assed twit
Incontinent oaf
What on earth was I thinking?"

So said the Chief of Foxes.

THE SONG THE BLACK FOX SANG

The black fox is an evil, dreadful, and vividly described creature,
until he challenges the folk hero Okikirmui, and meets an equally
dreadful and vividly described fate.

Okikirmui, or Okikurumi, is the quintessential Ainu hero,
descended directly from heaven, tirelessly defending mankind
against starvation and other troubles.

Haikunterke Haikoshitemturi
On the rocky headlands of our land
On the rocky headlands of the gods
I was sitting.
One day I went out and saw
The sea stretching away broad and calm, and on the sea
Okikirmui, Shupunramka and Samayunkur[17]
Had sailed out together to hunt for whales, and when I saw this
The evil heart I bear swelled with malice.

Over these rocks
Over the rocky headlands of our land
Over the rocky headlands of the gods
I ran from top to bottom
I ran with light feet and sinuous body
I barked with a low sound like heavy wood splintering.
I stared at the fountainhead of the river, and called to the storm

---

[17] Okikirmui is the most important of all Ainu heroes, wise and brave. There are
innumerable stories about him. By comparison, at least, Samayunkur is shallow,
indecisive, and weak. Shupunranka is the oldest of the three and is known for
mildness and reticence – which is why he appears in no stories of his own. [Chiri]

demon within.
And a violent wind, a whirling wind came forth from the spring
And blew on the ocean. And straightaway
The surface of the sea plunged down
And the depths of the sea rose up. Okikirmui's boat,
Caught where the coastal waters meet the ocean waters
In dire peril, in the space between the waves
Span round and round. Mountains of water
Wrapped around the boat. but
Okikirmui, Samayunkur and Shupunramka
Chanting loudly, kept on rowing.
That tiny boat was blown around like a fallen leaf
Almost already it seemed to capsize, but
Those brave Ainu nobly sent their little boat
Skipping through the wind
Slipping over the tops of the waves.

And when I saw this, the evil heart I bear swelled with malice.
I ran with light feet and sinuous body
I barked with a low sound like heavy wood splintering.
I urged the storm demon onward with all my strength
And as I did so, at last, Samayunkur
With blood running from the palms of his hands
And blood running from the backs of his hands
Collapsed from exhaustion
And a secret laugh bubbled up inside me.
Once more, with all my strength
I ran with light feet and sinuous body
Barking with a sound like heavy wood splintering.
I cheered on the storm demon.
Okikirmui and Shupunranka
Shouting encouragement to each other, were bravely rowing
onward, but
After a while Shupunramka
With blood running from the palms of his hands
And blood running from the backs of his hands

Collapsed from exhaustion
And again I laughed to myself.
I jumped up and ran about gracefully, with light feet
I barked with a sound like hard wood splintering –
But Okikirmui was still not even looking tired.
With only a thin garment round his body
He rowed onward until
The oar snapped in his hands.
At which he sprang over to half-dead Samayunkur
Snatched from him his oar
And rowed onward single-handed.

And when I saw this, the evil heart I bear swelled with malice.
Barking with a deep sound like hard wood splintering,
I ran with light feet and sinuous body
I urged on the storm demon with yet more force.
And soon the oar taken from Samayunkur, too,
Snapped in half. Okikirmui leapt over to Shupunranka
And seizing his oar rowed bravely onward
But this oar too was broken by the waves.
Then Okikirmui stood up in the middle of the boat,
Hero among humans, and though I did not believe
His eyes could search me out, yet
On the rocky headlands of our land
On the rocky headlands of the gods
His eyes stared straight into mine.
In his calm face the color of anger appeared,
He searched for something in his bag[18]
And I saw him draw out a little wormwood bow
And a little wormwood arrow.[19]

---

[18] The Ainu used bags woven from rushes when travelling on land, but this bag is made of sealskin or bearskin for use at sea. [Chiri]

[19] Wormwood arrows were favored on journeys because of their efficacy against demons, as we see here.

Seeing that, I laughed to myself.
"What is the so-called human doing? Trembling in fear of me?
What does he hope to use that feeble arrow for?"
On the rocky headlands of our land
On the rocky headlands of the gods
I ran up and down with light steps
I ran up and down gracefully.
I barked with a deep sound like heavy wood splintering.
I heaped praises upon the storm demon.
Meanwhile Okikirmui's arrow came flying
It hit me exactly in the back of the neck, it went right through...
What happened after that I could not tell.

When I came to,
The weather was good, and the surface of the sea
Was wide and calm, and Okikirmui's boat was gone.
From the top of my head to my feet
I was in agony, as if my skin were burning and shrinking.
I could never have thought that little arrow of the humans
Could make so much pain. With my limbs twisted in torment
Over these rocks
Over the rocky headlands of our land
Over the rocky headlands of the gods
I screamed with pain,
I writhed with pain,
By day and by night,
Half alive and half dead,
Until finally somehow I lost consciousness.
When I came round again,
I was sitting between the ears of a great black fox.
After two days, Okikirmui returned
He came with the appearance of a god, and grinning from ear to
ear he said,
"Mm, a fine sight to see –
The black fox god who keeps watch
Over the rocky headlands, the rocky headlands of the gods

Because he has a good heart, a godly heart
Dies a good and splendid death."
So saying, he took hold of my head
With vast strength he took my upper jawbone
And made out of it a latrine; my lower jaw
He made into a latrine for his wife;
And my body he left to rot in the earth.
And thus tortured by night and day
By the horrible stench
I died a pointless death, a horrible death.

I was not content to be a minor god;
Because of the evil heart I bore there was no choice –
I died a horrible death. Therefore,
Foxes of the ages to come, learn from my fate:
Never harbor wicked thoughts.
So said the fox god.

THE SONG THE RABBIT SANG

To a modern reader the rabbit's punishment and the generally dramatic tone of this *kamui yukar* might seem rather out of proportion to the crime, which was only to break traps. Breaking traps, however, means endangering the food supply and compromising the commerce between man and *kamui*.

Sampaya Terke
Running through valley after valley
I'd follow my big brother up to the mountains, playing together.
Every day I'd follow him, and sometimes
There'd be crossbow traps set by the humans[20]
And he would break them and I would always laugh.
But one day, out of the blue,
Suddenly my big brother was shouting and screaming –
He'd been caught by a trap.
I was horrified and ran to his side
And through his pain he said:

"Little brother, right now
You have to run quickly
When you get back to our village
Shout as loudly as you can:
MY BROTHER'S BEEN CAUGHT BY A TRAP!"

I heard him,
I said "Yes sir,"
Running through valley after valley

---

[20] The trap is a *yuwari*, a rather sophisticated trap used by the Ainu which consists of a crossbow firing a barbed harpoon into any unlucky animal that triggers it.

I arrived back at our village.
There, I remembered what my big brother had told me to do
I prepared my very loudest voice
But the words he'd told me to say
Had somehow completely slipped my mind. I stood around
Trying to think what they could have been, but it was useless.
And so once more
Running through valley after valley
I hopped all the way back again
But when I got back to where I'd left my big brother
There was nobody –
Only the marks of my brother's blood.

(Here, the action shifts to the older rabbit)

Ketka woiwoi ketka, ketka woiwoi ketka
Every day I'd go up into the mountains
Breaking the humans' crossbow traps;
That was just the normal way to amuse myself.
One day I found a crossbow trap set in my path
But just next to it there had also been set
A little crossbow made of wormwood.
I said to myself,
"Whatever does this do?"
And because it was so unusual
I thought I'd try touching it and running away.
And completely unawares
I was utterly caught in the trap
Beyond any hope of escape.
The more I struggled to get free
The tighter it gripped me – there was nothing I could do.[21]
I wept, and someone came running to my side –

---

[21] There might be some confusion in the original story between different kinds of trap; snares were used as well as *yuwari*.

My little brother. I was overjoyed; I gave him a message
For our family, to come and help.
But no matter how long I waited, no-one came.
I wept again and someone came to me –
A human appeared. He was a youth
As beautiful as a god, smiling broadly.
He picked me up and took me away
To a big house, filled with sacred treasures.
That young man built a fire,
He prepared a great iron pot, he took down a cleaver
He cut my body apart as if he were slicing leather
Filled the pot with me, and under it
He lit the fire.
I was desperate to escape,
I searched for some kind of weak spot in this man;
There was none, and not for a second
Did he take his eyes off me.
"The pot will boil and I will boil inside it,
Whatever I do I'll die a pointless death, a horrible death,"
I thought. I waited for the young man to do something careless,
And at last, in the form of a slice of my own flesh,
I scrambled up, reached the rim, and concealed by steam,
Jumped down onto the left-hand seat,
Threw myself quickly through the door,
Fled breathlessly, weeping as I ran
Back to my own village
Where I calmed myself down.

Looking back on it,
What I thought was just a human, just a youth,
Was surely Okikirmui, godlike in strength.
That's who it was, all right.
By disarming his traps every day
Thinking an ordinary human had set them
I had angered Okikirmui, making him set
His wormwood arrows against me.

But as I am no mere insignificant god,
And because it would be a shame if I died
A pointless death, a horrible death,
He took pity on me
And when I fled he did not pursue me.
And thus, ever since,
Because I couldn't resist meddling,
Whereas rabbits were as big as deer before
We've become as small as a single slice of meat.
All of my kind from now on
Are going to have to be as small as this.
Therefore, rabbits of the future, take heed not to make mischief!

So said the Chief of Rabbits as he died.

THE SONG THE MARSH DEMON SANG

A violent and exciting battle in which Okikirmui is aided by
Apehuchi, a major goddess in charge of fire and the hearth.
Because the dead are associated with the hearth, she also controls
the gateway between the living, the dead, and the *kamui* and has
many profound roles to play. In this particular story, though, she
seems to function as artillery support for Okikirmui.

Harit Kunna
One day, the weather was so nice
That I poked just my eyes and mouth
Out from the marsh; and from the direction of the beach
I found I could clearly hear human voices.
I saw that two young men were coming;
The one in front was like a hero,
Equipped with a hero's trappings,
As beautiful as a god, but the one behind
Had an unpleasant look and an unhealthy face.
Along they went, talking between themselves,
But as they passed in front of my marsh,
Just as they were right in front of me,
The unpleasant-looking one stopped dead and held his nose.

"Argh, what a stink! What foul marsh,
What revolting bog are we passing? How filthy!
What could make such a horrible smell?"
He said.

Just to hear this,
I was so enraged I hardly knew where I was.
I leapt up from the mud. Where I leapt
The ground cracked,

The ground was torn apart.
Baring my fangs, I plunged toward them,
But the one in front saw me in time,
Turned round like a fish flipping over,
Ducked around the unhealthy looking one
And got clean away.
The other one lasted for a couple of seconds
Before I caught up with him and swallowed him head first.

So, I chased the first man,
Which took every atom of strength I had,
Until we arrived at a human village, a big one.
And there coming right at me
Was old Grandma Fire,
Apehuchi the hearth goddess in six red robes
Tied up with a sash; in six red robes, a coat
And a red cane she ran up to me, saying:

"What's this? What's this? What are you up to,
Barging into a village? Off you go! Off you go!"

And she waved her red cane, her metal cane,
And struck me with it, and flames shot up from it
And fell on me like rain.
But I didn't care at all,
Clashing my fangs I continued my pursuit
I chased that man round and round the village in circles.
Where I ran,
The earth itself cracked,
The earth itself was torn apart.
The village was in an turmoil
Men pulling their wives along by the hand,
Men pulling their children along,
People crying and yelling and running away
Milling about like boiling water.
But I didn't care at all.

Raising a blizzard of earth
The old fire goddess rushed at me again
And terrible flames filled the air around me,
And meanwhile that man
Rushed into a house, and rushed back out again.
When I looked I saw,
He was fitting a little wormwood arrow to a little wormwood
bow
And grinning widely he took aim at me
Which I found rather amusing:
"With a little arrow like that, how will he do any damage?"
I said to myself, and clashing my fangs
I was about to swallow him head first,
When he shot me through the throat.

And from that point
I remember nothing.
When I regained consciousness,
I found myself between the ears of a great dragon.
The villagers were gathered, and the one I had chased
Was giving orders in a loud voice,
To cut my corpse into shreds,
To carry the remains away,
To burn them to ashes,
To scatter the ashes among the mountain rocks.
Then I realized for the first time, that was no ordinary man;
What I thought was an ordinary youth was actually
Okikirmui, the godlike hero.
Because a terrible and evil god, a demon, myself,
Had dwelt too near a human village,
Okikirmui, thinking of the good of the village, had punished me
Had tricked me into pursuing him, had killed me with his
wormwood arrows.
And then I realized that the man I swallowed
The sickly man, who I had thought was a human being,
Was actually Okikirmui's excrement, which he had formed into a

man
And then led to me.
Because I was an evil spirit,
I have been taken to the awful land of Hell
And in the world of humans there is no danger now
No lurking threat.
Although I was a terrible demon,
The cunning of just one man defeated me
And now I die a pointless death, a horrible death.

So said the Marsh Demon.

The Song The Wolf Cub Sang

Presented in book form, all these tales begin with a title that indicates exactly who is speaking. Originally, however, they were identified by their *sakehe* (the refrain) and the listener was left to guess what sort of being might be speaking. In this case, the speaker is revealed only at the very end, but the howl-like sound of the *sakehe* may be considered a clue.

Hotenao
One day, I was bored so I went to the beach
And I saw a human boy coming, so I played a game:
When he went downstream, I went downstream,
When he came upstream, I came upstream and blocked his way.
When we'd been downstream six times
And upstream six times,
Anger started to show on the boy's face and he said:

"*Pii tuntun, pii tuntun*
You little brat, if you're going to be like that
Tell me the names,
The past and present names,
Of this headland."

Hearing that, I laughed and replied:
"Is there anyone who doesn't know
The past and present names of this place?
Long ago, magnificent gods and men were here
And this headland was called 'The Headland of the Gods'.
But now in this age of decay
It's called only 'The Headland of *Inau*'!"

So I said, and he replied:

"*Pii tuntun, pii tuntun*
If that's your answer, kid,
Then try telling me the names,
The past and present names,
Of this river."

And what I said was,
"Is there anyone who doesn't know
The past and present names of this river?
Long ago, in the ages of glory,
This river was called 'The Swift-Flowing River'.
But now that the world has declined
It's called only 'The Slow-Flowing River'!"

So I said, and he replied:
"*Pii tuntun, pii tuntun*
If that's really your answer,
Then perhaps you can give an explanation
Of our own ancestry!"

This was my answer,
"Is there anyone who doesn't know your history?
Long, long ago, Okikirmui went up into the mountains
And when he built himself a shelter, he put in a hearth-frame of
hazelwood –
But when the fire was lit, the wood dried out
And warped so much that when Okikirmui trod on one end,
The other would go up in the air.
And that annoyed him so much
That he took the whole structure to the river
And threw it in.
So the wood drifted in the current
And reached the sea, where the gods noticed it
Being battered at random by the waves;
They thought it an unbearable shame
That the work of great Okikirmui

Should be drifting aimlessly, uselessly, rotting in the water
And so they turned that wood into a fish
And it was called *Inunpepecheppo*, the fire-fish.
As it happens, that same fire-fish
Knowing nothing of its origin
Is now wandering about in the form of a human being.
And that fire-fish is you!"
As I was speaking, the boy listened
With strong emotions following one another across his face.
"*Pii tuntun, pii tuntun*
Well you, you are a little wolf cub!"

As soon as he'd said that,
He plunged into the sea with a splash.
Where he vanished, a single red fish
With great strokes of its tail
Could be seen swimming away to the open sea.

So said the young wolf god.

THE SONG THE OWL GOD SANG: "KONKUWA"

The narrator here is Chikap Kamui, the owl god. This is the most important *yukar* about him, and describes the covenant between *kamui* and human beings, taught by Chikap Kamui so that people will not go hungry.

Hunting was seen as an exchange between humans and *kamui* whereby the human would obtain the dead body of the animal inhabited by the *kamui*, who in turn would receive decorations and *inau* which they could bring back to *kamui moshir*, the spirit world. To kill fish and deer, if it is done with correct protocols, is thus to make a mutually agreeable bargain with the *kamui*.

Konkuwa
"Long ago, when I spoke
It was like the sound of a strong bow
Bound with cherry bark
Plucked just in the very center;
But now I have weakened and grown old.
If only there were someone with eloquence
Someone having the confidence to be my messenger
I could give them the task
Of taking the Five-and-a-Half Petitions to Heaven."

Thus I spoke,
While tapping the head of my drum.
Somone appeared at the door, saying
"Well, nobody's more eloquent
Or more confident a messenger than me, right?"
And I saw it was a young crow.
I asked him in, and then,
While tapping the head of my drum,
To make the young crow my messenger

I recited the Petitions to him for three days.
As I was reciting the Petitions of the third day, I looked
And the young crow was taking a nap by the hearth.
Seeing this, I was convulsed with righteous rage
And I beat that sack of feathers until he died.

And once more
While tapping the head of my drum
I chanted
"Whoever has the confidence to be my messenger,
I wish to charge him with the task
Of taking the Five-and-a-Half Petitions to Heaven."

Someone appeared at the door, saying,
"Other than me, could anyone be found
Eloquent enough to handle the job? I think not."
And I saw it was a mountain jay.
I invited him in and once again
While tapping the head of my drum
I recited to him the Five-and-a-Half Petitions.
Four days went by, and as I enumerated the fourth day's tasks,
The mountain jay took a nap by the fire.
Furious, I beat that sack of feathers until he died.

And once more
While tapping the head of my drum
I chanted
"If anyone is eloquent and confident
Enough to be my messenger,
I wish him to carry the Five-and-a-Half Petitions to Heaven."

With excellent manners and self-control
Someone came in, and I saw it was a dipper;
With flawless etiquette he seated himself
In the left-hand seat. Once again
While tapping the head of my drum

I expounded the Five-and-a-half Petitions,
Speaking by night and by day without pause.
When I looked, the young dipper
Showed no signs of tiredness.
He listened both night and day
Until the sixth day, when I finished speaking,
And at once he flew out by the skylight
And headed toward Heaven.
The chief import of the Petitions was this:
That in the world of men, the people were even now
About to die of starvation. And the reason was
That the god in charge of deer, and the god in charge of fish
Had agreed together that they would send
No deer and no fish. And the humans,
Whatever the gods told them to do,
Would just look blank; and so
When they went hunting in the hills, there were no deer
When they went fishing in the rivers, there were no fish.
It was because this situation angered me
That I had sent a messenger to the gods of deer and fish.

Many days passed, and from the sky
I heard a faint sound as if someone was coming.
I saw the young dipper, who now with a more beautiful bearing,
A more refined dignity even than before,
Recited Heaven's reply.

The gods of deer and fish
Had been refusing to send deer or send fish
For this reason: When humans caught a deer,
They would club it to death, flay its skin
And throw the head away to lie in the woods,
And when they caught a fish
They would club it to death with rotten wood.
And so the deer returned to their god naked and crying
And the fish returned to their god carrying rotten wood.

The gods of deer and fish, angry, had consulted together
And decided for these reasons to send no deer or fish.
But they also declared clearly
That if the humans would treat the fish and deer courteously,
Then deer could be sent again, fish could be sent again.

Hearing this, I heaped praise on the dipper,
And quickly checking I found that indeed
The treatment of deer and fish taken by humans
Was rough and displeasing.
Therefore, so that this behavior would cease,
While they slept I appeared to the humans in dreams
And taught them, until even they
Understood the problem. And from then on
Tools for catching fish were made as beautiful as an *inau*,
And when deer were caught, the heads were decorated and revered,
And thus the fish, carrying beautiful *inau*,
Would return happily to the god of fish,
And the deer, heads elegantly trimmed,
Would return happily to the god of deer.
And the happy deer god and fish god gladly sent
Multitudes of fish, multitudes of deer.

And the humans now lived their lives
Without danger, without hunger,
And seeing this I was content.
For I am already old, already weak,
And I am already thinking of going to heaven
And though I could not leave while the world I protect,
The world of humans, is menaced by famine
While the people are dying of hunger,
Yet now my worries have abated,
And leaving the strongest, the young heroes
To look after the world of humans,
Now at last I am about to go to Heaven.

So said the Owl God, the protector of the land
As he ascended to Heaven.

THE SONG THE SEA GOD SANG

This long story is a critique of the covenant between human beings and food-providing *kamui*. In this case, the food source is beached whales, which are provided by the sea god, Repun Kamui. Repun Kamui is a rather cheerful *kamui* who seems to trust humans to treat his gifts respectfully.

This tale does not easily give away the identity of the narrator; but many clues are given from which the listener can eventually learn that Repun Kamui here has the form of a killer whale.

Repun Kamui is often depicted in this form. However, like all *kamui* who adopt an animal body in this world, he looks and behaves like a human when at his home in *kamui moshir* and indeed hunts whales himself.

> *Atuika tomaomaki kuntuteshi hm hm*
> Tall brothers, six brothers, tall sisters, six sisters,
> Short brothers, six brothers, short sisters, six sisters,
> Here is how I was raised:
> Near where the treasures were piled, a dais was provided;
> Sitting on that dais, carving new knife-sheaths:
> That was how my days were spent.
>
> Every day, when morning came the brothers
> Took their quivers on their backs, and departed with the sisters;
> When twilight came, with tired faces
> Empty-handed the sisters returned
> Tired though they were they prepared a meal, offered me a tray
> And they too ate, and cleared up, and
> The brothers then employed their hands busily in making arrows.

When the quivers were full again, everyone was so tired
That they slept with mighty snores that echoed around.

When the next day came, once again, while it was still dark,
Everyone got up, and once again the sisters made food and
offered me my tray
Everyone finished their meal, and once again took their quivers
on their backs
And out they went. And once again, when evening came
With empty hands and tired faces they came back
The sisters prepared a meal, the brothers prepared arrows
Always it was the same thing.

One day, the brothers and the sisters
Took up the quivers and went out.
I who had been making carved treasures, finally
Got up from the dais, to my little golden bow
Fitting my little golden arrows, and I went outside.
I saw that far and wide the sea was calm
And from the eastern sea to the western, the whales
Were playing, splash splash! Then, in the east
Tall sisters, six sisters joined their hands to make a ring,
Short sisters, six sisters, chased the whales into the ring,
Tall brothers, six brothers, short brothers, six brothers,
Aimed and fired at the whales in the ring,
And the arrows passed above the whales and below the whales.
Every day, they must have been doing this!
I saw that in the center of the ocean
A huge whale, a parent and child, up and down
Splash splash, could be seen playing, so
From a distance,
I fitted a little gold arrow to the little gold bow,
Took aim and fired, and with a single arrow
I shot through both parent and child.

There, splitting one whale down the middle,

I took half of it, and into the ring of sisters
I hurled it. Then placing the whale-and-a-half
Under my tail, I headed for the land of humans
To the village of Otashut;
I cast the whale-and-a-half
Up on the village beach.
And having done so, diving lazily into the sea
I swam back home.
As soon as I arrived, somebody
Came running, out of breath.
I looked and it was a sea-wren.
And out of breath, it gasped:

"*Tominkarikur Kamuikarikur Isoyankekur*
Valorous God, Great God,
For what possible reason have you,
For mere humans, for horrible humans,
Offered this great bounty of the sea?
Mere humans, horrible humans, axes in hand,
Sickles in hand, are chopping, are jabbing,
Are carving and slicing this great gift;
O brave God, O Great God, make haste
And withdraw your sea-bounty!
Even for such an extravagant bounty
Mere humans, horrible humans,
Will feel no gratitude!"

So it said, and I, laughing, replied:

"Since this is something I have decided to bestow on the humans,
Since it's theirs now and not mine, the humans
May slice it with sickles, may chop it with axes
May consume it entirely or whatever they want;
They have a right to eat what is theirs, do they not?
Is that all right with you?"

The sea-wren loitered around, but
Not caring about it whatsoever,
Lazily diving in and out of the sea, I swam slowly away
And before twilight came, I reached
My own sea. I saw that
The twelve brothers and the twelve sisters,
Instead of hauling their half-whale home,
Had raised their voices to the eastern sea, and were loudly
complaining.
At this point I gave up on them completely.
Not caring about them whatsoever,
To my house I returned and sat down on the dais.
There, looking back at the world of humans, I saw
The whale-and-a-half that I had cast up
Was surrounded by splendid men and
Splendid women in magnificent clothes,
Dancing with happiness, leaping with joy, and on the sandy
beach
Rich rugs were laid, and on them stood the *nispa* of the village of
Otashut;
Wearing six robes, binding with a sash six robes,
A holy crown, an ancestral crown, on his head,
Girding on the sword of divine right
Raising his hands high in worship
In a manner as beautiful as a god's. With loud cries
The people rejoiced in the sea's bounty.

That stupid seagull had said that the humans
would hack at my gift with their axes, but instead
The chief first
Took up a long-revered sword
Greatest of the village's treasures,
And with that he cut and apportioned the meat.

Still, my brothers and sisters
showed no sign of returning.

After two or three days, at the window
Something could be seen, and
Turning to look closely, on the east window
I saw a golden dish overflowing
With salmon, and on top
An *inau* and ritual chopsticks were stood[22]
As a messenger, which carried back and forth this message:[23]

"On behalf of the people of Otashut
In a spirit of reverence I offer this ritual sake."

As the representative
Of the *nispa* and people of Otashut
It uttered a prayer of thanks to me
whose burden was thus:

"*Tominkarikur Kamuikarikur Isoyankekur*
Great god, valorous god
Our village suffered a famine
So bad that nothing could be done.
When there was no food you took pity on us.
You gave life to our village for which
We offer the deepest thanks, we rejoice in the sea's bounty
Brewing a modicum of sake, adding a small inau,
Our thanks to the great god
We humbly express."

With which, an *inau*-topped portion of sake
Was offered.

---

[22] Chopsticks decorated with little *inau* were used when offering sake to the gods. This '*kike-ush-pashi*', acting as a sort of agent, goes to the place of the gods when people have something they would like to say, and delivers the message. [Chiri]

[23] The Japanese has 'corpse' rather than 'messenger' – these words happen to sound the same, and this is probably a mistake in the Japanese text.

Thereupon I rose, took the golden dish,
Accepted the offering,
Uncovered the six sake barrels at the high seat
Added the liquor bit by bit
And placed the dish over the window.
When this was done, I rested on the dais.
I saw that the dish had vanished along with the chopsticks. Then,
I went back to carving knife-sheaths, decorating knife-sheaths...
After a while, happening to look around, I saw
The house was full of beautiful *inau*
The house was full of white swirling clouds, with white lighting
Sparkling and flashing. "How beautiful," I thought.

After that, two or three days went by
And at last, the brothers
and sisters with loud voices
came hauling their whale homeward.
I had no more patience for them.
Seeing what was inside the house,
The brothers and sisters were terrified, and their faces drooped.
Everyone came in and saw all the *inau*
And in shock they prostrated themselves again and again
Meanwhile, the six sake barrels at the east seat
Were overflowing, so that sake (beloved of the gods!)
Flowed through the house.
Then I decorated the inside of the house with lovely *inau*
And gods from far and near I invited
And gave a great banquet. The sisters
Boiled whalemeat and served it up
And the assembled gods smacked their lips with pleasure.
When the party was at its height i got up
And told the tale of how I,
Concerned lest there be famine in the world of humans
Caused sea-bounty to be cast ashore;
And of how the envious gull complained, and how

The chief of Otashut spoke grateful words,
Raised prayers to me, sent a messenger in the form of
Sake and inau with pleasing words, and the assembled gods
Spoke as with one voice
Praising me.
Then returning to the feast
The company raised a clamour of dancing and leaping
With my sisters passing among them as cup-bearers
Voices raised in beautiful song.

Two or three days passed and the feast ended.
Each god took two or three beautiful inau
And bowing at the waist prostrated themselves again and again
And all returned to their own houses.
Since that time, without fail,
Whenever people make sake
They send sake and inau to me and my
Tall brothers, six brothers
Tall sisters, six sisters
Short brothers, six brothers,
Short sisters, six sisters.

And now, with no shortage of food
With no troubles to beset them
People live their tranquil lives;
And my mind is at peace.

THE SONG THE FROG SANG

This *yukar* is pure comedy. Even so, it serves to reassure the
listener that even humans have their rights and prerogatives that
the *kamui* must respect.

Tororo hanrok, hanrok!
One day, as I was hopping over the plains
As I amused myself, what should I see
But a house! So I went to the door and peeped in,
And in the house the dais was piled with treasures!
And on the dais there was a young man
Who was bent over, carefully whittling
A sheath for a knife, so I thought I'd play a little trick on him,
And I came and sat on the threshold and bellowed

"TORORO HANROK HANROK!"

But the young man just lifted up his knife hand
And looked at me and chuckled:
"Do I hear a solemn recitation? Or do I hear a joyful ditty?
Ah, if only I could hear more!"
So I was quite pleased and once more I bellowed

"TORORO HANROK HANROK!"

At which the young man said:
"Do I hear you sing a *yukar*?
Or do I hear a *sakehaw*?[24]
Ah, how I wish I could hear it from close up!"

---

[24] A type of boisterous drinking song that would be hard to mistake for a *yukar*.

So I was rather flattered and I hopped up
Onto the lower seat by the hearth and I bellowed

"TORORO HANROK HANROK!"

And the young man said:
"Do I hear you sing a noble *yukar*?
 Or do I hear a boisterous *sakehaw*?
Ah, how I wish I could hear it from even closer!"
So I was overjoyed and I hopped up
To the high seat, where I bellowed

"TORORO HANROK HANROK!"

When suddenly! Wham! He jumped up
Brandishing a big burning stick from the fire –
Hurled it at me – there was a horrible sort of crunch –
And that's when I lost consciousness.

When I came to
There was a big rubbish pile, and on the very top
Was lying a big fat dead frog, and I was sitting between its ears.
Now that I think of it, what I thought was an ordinary house
Was actually that of Okikirmui, godlike in strength,
And I had tried to play a trick
Not realizing that it was Okikirmui himself.
And now I die a pointless death, a horrible death,

And therefore, frogs of the future,
Without fail, refrain from taunting humans!
So said a fat frog, and then expired.

A SONG PON OKIKIRMUI SANG

Pon means 'small', and so Pon Okikirmui is Okikirmui as a child. Stories focusing on Okikirmui were sometimes presented as being about Pon Okikirmui, so as to avoid disrespect. Even as a child, however, Okikirmui ferociously upholds the covenant between man and *kamui*, and thus defends the food supply.

Kutnisa kutunkutun
One day I went for a walk up the river
And by the spring I saw a boy
Hard at work, bending over in the water,
Hammering in stakes for a walnut-wood fish trap.
Seeing me, what he said was:

"Who are you? Come here, friend, and give me a hand with this."
I saw that because the stakes were walnut-wood
Walnut-colored water, muddy water
Came flowing out, and the salmon
Came out of the water and because they hated the muddy water
Were returning, weeping, to their homes. I was angry
And therefore, I grabbed the hammer that the boy was holding
And the sound of the blows I gave him echoed around.
I struck him so hard his hips broke, I killed him,
I sent him to Hell. Judging by the shaking
Of those walnut stakes, he reached
The bottom of the sixth Hell.
And then, I put forth the strength of my body,
I exerted my power, I snapped those stakes
At the very base, and sent them, too, to Hell.

From the spring came a clean wind, a clean water

Came flowing forth.
The salmon recovered with the clean wind and water
With loud rejoicing and laughter,
They jumped up and down.
Seeing this, my mind was at rest,
And I walked back home along the river.
So said the young Okikirmui.

ANOTHER SONG PON OKIKIRMUI SANG

Nitnekamui is the chief evil *kamui*. His attempt to disrupt the
ecological balance between man and beasts is foiled by Okikirmui.

Tanota hurehure
One day, as I was taking a walk downstream,
I met Pon Nitnekamui, the devil.
The devil always has a beautiful appearance,
A beautiful face. Dressed in black,
Carrying a little walnut bow and little walnut arrows
With a smile he said:
"Okikirmui, let's play a game.
Now I'm going to show you how to make fish extinct."

So saying, he fitted a walnut arrow to his walnut bow,
And fired an arrow toward the spring
And from the spring came walnut water, cloudy water
Flowed out, and when the salmon came
The filthy water hurt them and weeping
They returned to their homes and Pon Nitnekamui
Smiled brightly at this.
But I was angered at the sight,
I fitted a gold arrow to the golden bow I carried,
I fired an arrow toward the spring
And from the spring came silvery water, clean water
Flowed out, and the salmon that had fled
Were healed by the clean water
And with loud laughter and merriment
Went splashing up the river.
Pon Nitnekamui, his face filled with rage, said:
"Well, if you insist on this, I'm going to show you how to make deer
extinct."

And fitting a walnut arrow to his walnut bow
He aimed at the sky itself, and from the high plains
A walnut wind, a whirlwind came blowing,
And from the high plains, herd by herd,
The deer were blown clean up into the sky.
Pon Nitnekamui smiled brightly.
But I was furious at the sight,
 I fitted a gold arrow to the golden bow,
 I fired it after the deer,
And from the heavens
A silver wind, a clean wind came blowing down,
And herd by herd, the deer were blown back down
To the high plains.
Pon Nitnekamui, his face filled with anger, said:
"You impertinent scum! If that's really how you want it,
Let's have a real contest."

And he took off his jacket.
I too stripped down to one thin garment
And we wrestled, he and I grappled together.
And then now falling, now rising again, we fought,
But I was appalled at his terrible strength.
But in the end, the time came
When using the strength of my hips, the might of my body, Every
bit, I lifted Pon Nitnekamui
Onto my shoulders, and the sound echoed all around
When I hurled him down onto the jagged rocks.
I killed him, I pushed him down into Hell,
And then all around there was silence.
When it was all over, I went home along the river,
And the loud laughter and merriment of the salmon
Came drifting to my ears, along with much splashing.
And from the high plains,
The loud laughter and merriment of the deer
Filled the air as they grazed on every side.

Seeing this, I was content,
And I went back home to my house.

So said Pon Okikirmui.

THE SONG THE OTTER SANG

A number of figures in Ainu lore appear sometimes more like gods and sometimes more like heroes. Samayunkur, who appeared as a human hero in an earlier tale, also has a more godlike aspect, Oina Kamui, who taught crafts to humanity. He therefore has no father or mother.

Kappa Reureu Kappa
One day, when I went for a swim along the stream,
I swam down to the place where Samayunkur draws water, and
Along came Samayunkur's little sister, looking as beautiful as a goddess,
Holding a bucket in one hand and in the other
A bundle of rushes. So putting just my head out
At the edge of the river, I said:
"Have you a father? Have you a mother?"

The startled maiden turned her eyes this way and that
Until she found me, and the color of anger
Appeared in her face.
"Oh, horrible flat-head, bad flat-head
Is showing no respect. [25]
Dogs! Get him!"
She said, and a pack of huge dogs
Came rushing up, clashing their fangs
When they saw me. I was surprised and I dove
To the bottom of the river, I fled
To the very bed of the river.

---

[25] The word she uses is *okapushpa*, which means to speak lightly of someone's dead relatives, or to reveal personal secrets. [Chiri]

Later, I came to where Okikirmui draws water
And putting just my head out at the mouth of the river
I saw Okikirmui's little sister, as beautiful as a goddess,
With a bucket in one hand and in the other
A bundle of rushes. And I said:
"Have you a father? Have you a mother?"

The startled maiden turned her eyes this way and that
Until she found me, and the color of anger
Appeared in her face.
"Oh, horrible flat-head, bad flat-head
Is showing no respect.
Dogs! Get him!"
She said, and a pack of huge dogs rushed at me.
Seeing that, I remembered what had happened just recently With a
scornful laugh I dived into the river
To make my escape. I had no idea that the dogs
Would do exactly the same thing – but clashing their fangs
They chased me to the very bottom of the river
They dragged me back up to the shore,
They ripped me with their teeth, they tore me with their teeth, And
in the end I lost consciousness.

When I came to, I was sitting between the ears of a big otter.
I had mocked Samayunkur and Okikirmui
Knowing that they had neither father nor mother
And my punishment was
To be killed by Okikirmui's dogs,
To die a pointless death, a horrible death.
Otters of the future, take care to behave yourselves!
So said the otter.

THE SONG THE MARSH MUSSEL SANG

We conclude with a touching story about shellfish. Samayunkur's sister falls short but Okikirmui's sister (who in another aspect is the goddess of tattooing) is kind.

Tonupeka ranran
Strong sunlight had dried out the place where I lived,
And I was in danger of death.
"Someone, please bring me water to drink,
Help me, I beg! Water, water!"
We all cried, and from the beach a woman came
With a basket on her back.
As we were crying out, she came past us,
Looked at us, and
"You stupid mussels, you bad mussels,
What are you bawling about,
Why are you making such a racket?" she said,
And she trod on us, and kicked us out of her way,
And crushed us in our shells, and went on her way
Up into the mountains.

"Ohhh, the pain! Water, water!"
We cried, and from the beach came another woman
With a basket on her back.
"Someone bring us water to drink! Help us!
Ohhh the pain! Water, water!!" we cried,
And with a manner as refined and beautiful as a god's,
She came over to us and said,
"Oh, poor things! In this heat,
The mussel beds are drying out, and they must need water,
And what's this? It's as if someone has been squashing them!"
She said as she gathered us all up in a big leaf

And put us down in a nice lake.
The clean, cold water revived us completely
And we glowed with health.

Now that we have had time to think about it,
The differences in disposition of these ladies
Tell us that the first, the one who trod on us,
That horrible woman, that nasty woman,
Was Samayunkur's little sister –
Whereas the one who took pity on us,
The young maid who helped us with such gracefulness,
Was Okikirmui's little sister.
Because Samayunkur's sister was so unpleasant,
Her millet fields dried out, but
Okikirmui's sister's fields prospered.
That year, Okikirmui's little sister had a plentiful harvest,
And knowing that it was thanks to us
She piled up millet ears in mussel shells.
And that is why every year, when women harvest millet,
They use mussel shells.

So said a marsh mussel.

CPSIA information can be obtained
at www.ICGtesting.com
Printed in the USA
LVHW101408030822
725074LV00002BA/217